# A Note to Parents

DK READERS is a compelling program for beginning readers, designed in conjunction with leading literacy experts, including Dr. Linda Gambrell, Director of the Eugene T. Moore School of Education at Clemson University. Dr. Gambrell has served on the Board of Directors of the International Reading Association and as President of the National Reading Conference.

Beautiful illustrations and superb full-color photographs combine with engaging, easy-to-read stories to offer a fresh approach to each subject in the series. Each DK READER is guaranteed to capture a child's interest while developing his or her reading skills, general knowledge, and love of reading.

The five levels of DK READERS are aimed at different reading abilities, enabling you to choose the books that are exactly right for your child:

**Pre-level 1:** Learning to read
**Level 1:** Beginning to read
**Level 2:** Beginning to read alone
**Level 3:** Reading alone
**Level 4:** Proficient readers

The "normal" age at which a child begins to read can be anywhere from three to eight years old, so these levels are only a general guideline.

No matter which level you select, you can be sure that you are helping your child learn to read, then read to learn!

D0289778

LONDON, NEW YORK, MUNICH,
MELBOURNE, and DELHI

**Series Editors** Deborah Lock, Penny Smith
**Art Editor** Jacqueline Gooden
**U.S. Editor** Elizabeth Hester
**DTP Designer** Almudena Díaz
**Production** Alison Lenane
**Jacket Designer** Hedi Gutt

### Reading Consultant
Linda Gambrell, Ph.D.

First American Edition, 2005
05 06 07 08 09 10 9 8 7 6 5 4 3 2 1
Published in the United States by DK Publishing, Inc.
375 Hudson Street, New York, New York 10014

DK books are available at special discounts for bulk purchases for sale promotions,
premiums, fundraising, or educational use. For details, contact:
DK Publishing Special Markets
375 Hudson Street
New York, NY 10014
SpecialSales@dk.com

Published in Great Britain by Dorling Kindersley Limited.

Library of Congress Cataloging-in-Publication Data

Lock, Deborah.
  Let's make music / written by Deborah Lock.-- 1st American ed.
    p. cm. -- (DK readers)
  ISBN 978-0-7566-1422-5 (pb) -- ISBN 978-0-7566-1423-2 (plc)
  1. Music--Instruction and study--Juvenile. I. Title. II. Dorling Kindersley readers.
  MT740.L75 2005
  372.87'3--dc22

                          2005009999

Color reproduction by Colourscan, Singapore
Printed and bound in the U.S.A. by Lake Book Manufacturing, Inc.

The publisher would like to thank the following for their kind permission
to reproduce their photographs:
a=above; c=center; b=below; l=left; r=right t=top

**Alamy Images:** Gabe Palmer III 4-5; Photofusion Picture Library/ Molly Cooper 15c;
Hemera Technologies 25bcl; image100 27; ImageDJ 29. **Corbis:** 10br; Ariel Skelley
28; Cat Gwynn 24-25; John Henley 30-31; Keren Su 7; Tom Stewart 16-17;
Wartenberg/Picture Press 14. **Early Learning Centre:** 7bcr, 10tl, 10bl, 11bl, 12br,
13cr, 13bl, 18bcr, 20br, 20t, 21br, 22c, 25bcr. **Getty Images:** Patrick Molnar 6; Sean
Murphy 26; Terry Vine 21. **Photolibrary.com:** Studio 10 - Scholastic 11.
**Zefa Visual Media:** E. Krenkel 18-19; Meeke 12t; R. Elstermann 9t; R.de Rooij 23.

All other images © Dorling Kindersley
For more information see: www.dkimages.com

Discover more at
# www.dk.com

**READERS**

LEARNING
pre-level
**1**
TO READ

# Let's Make Music

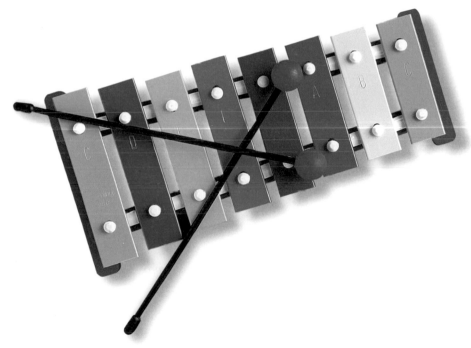

DK

DK Publishing, Inc.

trash
can lid

4

We play our instruments and make music together.

cymbal

cymbals

We crash the cymbals
and make a loud noise.

drumstick

drum

 drums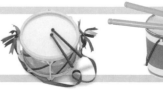

We bang
the drums
fast and slow.

bell

We shake
the bells
and make
them ring.

bells

xylophone

We hit the keys
on the xylophone
[ZY-lo-fone].

 xylophones

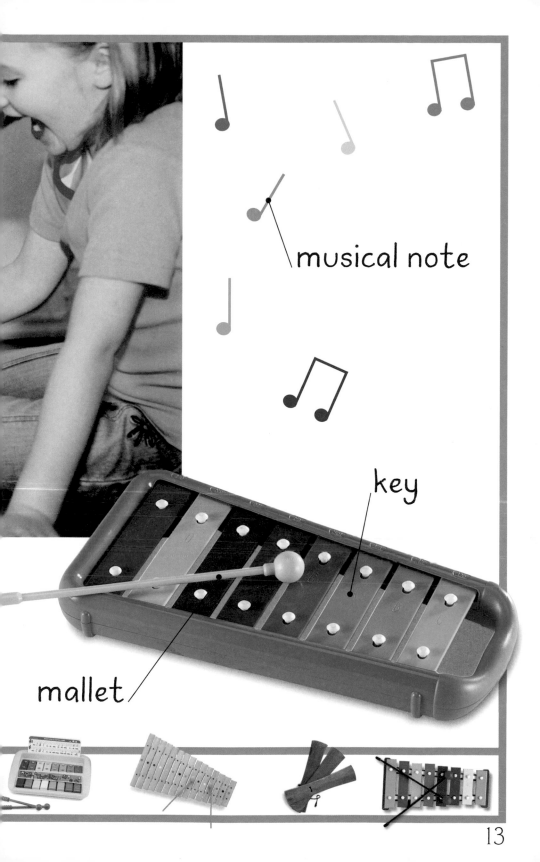

musical note

key

mallet

whistle

whistles

We blow our whistles
at the carnival.

carnival

I bang the pots and pans with spoons.

pots and pans

spoon

lid

17

I play high and
low notes
on the keyboard.

keyboards

accordion

cymbal

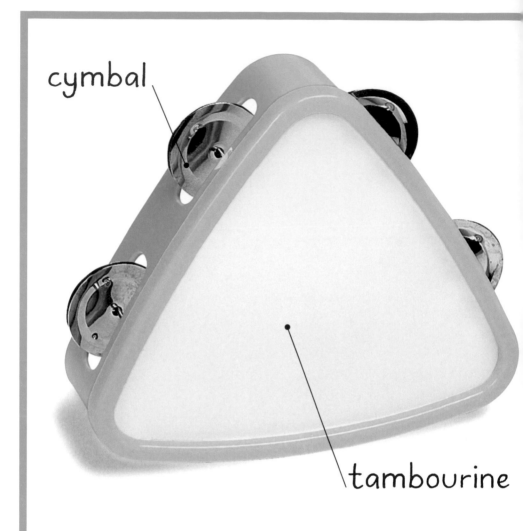

tambourine

I shake and tap
my tambourine.

 tambourines

21

I strum the strings
on my guitar.

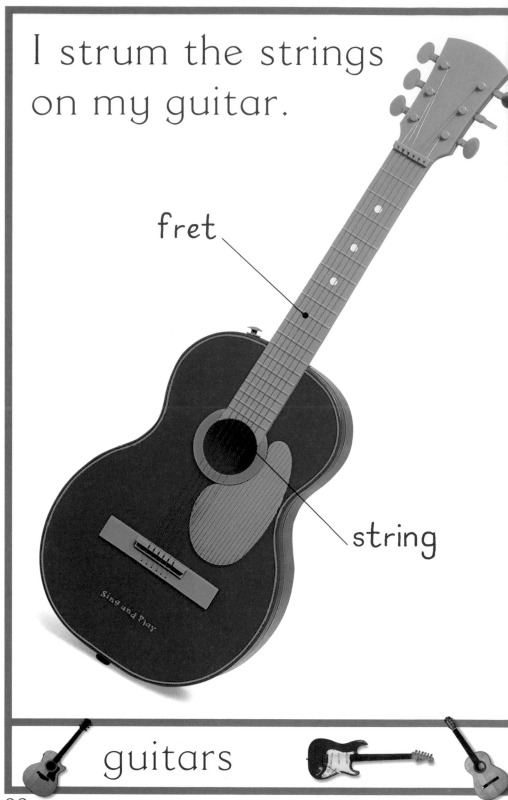

fret

string

guitars

guitar

23

I blow a tune on my harmonica.

harmonicas

harmonica

We clap our hands
and sing.

hands

hands

mouth

skipping

feet

# We move our feet and dance.

jumping

dancing

maracas

recorder

Let's play

ukulele

horn

music together.

# Picture word list

**cymbal**

page 6

**drum**

page 8

**bell**

page 10

**xylophone**

page 12

**whistle**

page 14

**pan**

page 16

**keyboard**

page 18

**tambourine**

page 20

**guitar**

page 22

**harmonica**

page 24

**hands**

page 26

**feet**

page 28